"I've never felt any lack of power. I feel if you do the thing you'll have the power. I'm limited only by whatever my talents are."

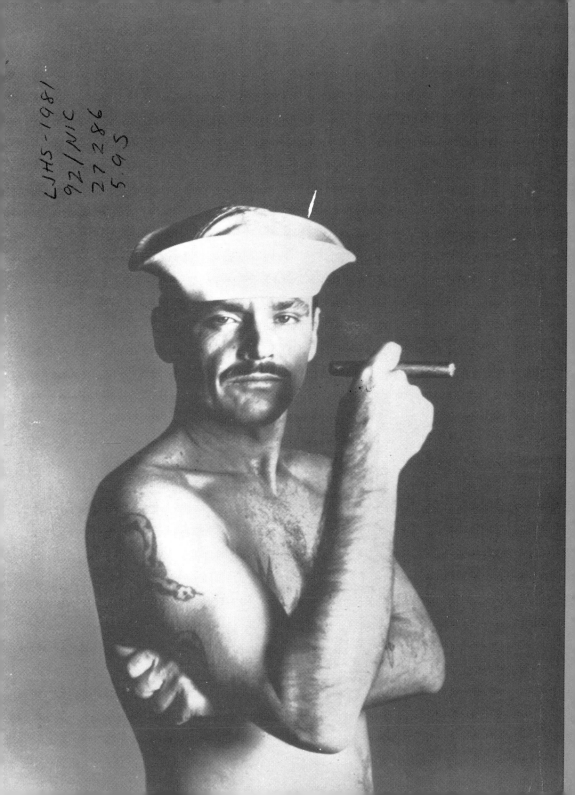

THE FILMS
OF
JACK NICHOLSON

Bruce Braithwaite

LARAMIE JUNIOR HIGH IMC

ISBN 0-912616-76-8

Greenhaven Press, Inc.
577 Shoreview Park Ave.
St. Paul, Minnesota 55112

"There are two ways up the ladder — hand over hand or scratching and clawing. It's sure been tough on my nails." But succeed he did, though in the beginning it looked more like blind faith than foresight. "When I went into films I aimed for stardom. I figured if you were going to act on the screen there was nothing much else to be, except a star." He waited a long time — over a decade — but in 1976 there was the final accolade for the man who wanted to be a star: the Oscar for Best Actor after a string of nominations. The film was, of course, *One Flew Over the Cuckoo's Nest* which cornered most of the awards that year. Jack Nicholson, perhaps the most unconventional of all superstars, could write his own ticket. The days of the B-picture had gone for good.

He was born in Neptune, New Jersey on April 22, 1937, the only son of John and Ethel May Nicholson. He has two older sisters, Lorraine and June. June left home when Jack was four to become a showgirl in Miami. Jack's father, a window dresser and sign painter, was an alcoholic and abandoned his wife and family soon after Jack's birth. Mrs Nicholson ran a beauty parlour from a room in the family home and business boomed. Soon they moved to a bigger establishment. It was, in many ways, a comfortable middle class upbringing. Young Jack was bright, able to skip a year in school without any trouble at all. He was funny, with, a school friend recalls, "a terrific smile." One he would later use, with devastating precision, in the movies.

At school he dabbled in dramatics, making his debut at ten singing "Managua Nicaragua" at the Roosevelt Grammar School. He was in the basketball team and had firm views, even then, on how the game should be played. On one occasion he suspected the rival team of cheating and decided to pay them back. He ruined the electrical equipment in their gym, confessed his crime and was suspended from school. To pay for the damage he took a part-time job.

He was gifted academically and it seemed logical that he would go on to University. Indeed he flirted with the idea of going to the University of Delaware, but hated the idea of further schooling. So he followed his sister, June, to Los Angeles and stayed. He was seventeen. He found a job as a messenger in the cartoon department at Metro-Goldwyn-Mayer. It paid thirty dollars a week, enough to abandon his idea of University forever. "I guess I wanted to see how films were made and get near movie stars." At that point he had no thoughts about being one of them. His own acting experience

Opposite: a scene from Studs Lonigan

at school had been more coercion than ambition. "I got sort of talked into it by a teacher. All the chicks I liked were doing plays."

While working as a messenger at MGM he made it a policy to address the executives by their first names. "Hi, Joe," he'd say to Joe Pasternak. One day Pasternak replied: "Hey, kid, how d'you like to be in pictures?" It didn't work out and even later a worried casting director told him: "I don't know what we'd ever use you for, but if we need you, we'll need you very badly."

But he did decide to take acting lessons and joined a group of would-be talents at an acting school run by Jeff Corey. His companions included James Coburn, Sally Kellerman, Roger Corman, Carol Eastman and Robert Towne. Nicholson and Towne became close friends and shared a cluttered apartment on the borders of Hollywood; they also lusted after the same girls at the acting school, apparently without much success, since the girls weren't interested in nobodies in a town full of somebodies. Those early colleagues all became successful and their careers continued to intertwine; the memories of bad times creating an umbilical link when the good times beckoned.

Nicholson's early experience was mainly in television and he

Opposite: in Ride the Whirlwind. Left: Five Easy Pieces.

Right: The Last Detail. Opposite: Easy Rider

never had more than a transitory interest in the theatre. Occasionally there would be an acting job in some small budget production: enough to pay the rent. "Some of the experiences were not happy, but once I had decided to take up acting professionally I never earned my living doing anything else. In the early days that meant if I was offered a part, the chances were I took it. That was the reality of my situation."

One of those fellow students, Roger Corman, gave Nicholson his first chance: a leading role in a sixty-minute thriller, *Cry Baby Killer*. It was 1958: Jack Nicholson, at twenty-one, was on his way. Corman had become a prolific producer-director of films which at the time were treated with some seriousness, but which he personally refers to as "Z movies." Mostly they were aimed at a voracious audience — the drive-in market. They were low budget pictures which made their money back at the drive-ins and foreign sales were not particularly courted. In *Cry Baby Killer*, Nicholson played a youth who commits a murder and holds out against the police in a storeroom with two hostages. His girlfriend (Carolyn Mitchell), finally talks him into giving himself up, just as the police are about to storm the building. His second film was

Too Soon To Love (GB: *Teenage Lovers*), a film about teenage promiscuity being the result of parental neglect.

Looking back on his early contribution to movies, Nicholson has in recent years commented wryly: "I either played the clean-cut boy next door, or the murderer of a family of at least five." These films included *The Wild Ride*, as a young tough who causes the deaths of several cops; *Broken Land*, as one of three young men unjustly jailed by a crooked sheriff; *Studs Lonigan*, as one of a group of teenagers living in the Depression era. This was his best film of the time and was screened during the London Film Festival. In *The Little Shop of Horrors* he played a young man who grows a man-eating plant mutation that can talk.

During this time he met an actress called Sandra Knight. They were married in 1961. "We were very much in love and I took the vows totally at ease." A year later Sandra, who had given up her career, gave birth to a daughter, Jennifer. The marriage foundered, but Nicholson sees his daughter regularly, while being careful not to pressure her. "I am tentative about infringing on Jenny's life. I want to be invited to enter her world, to be admitted gracefully." He has an ambivalent attitude to marriage and clearly does not contemplate another attempt. "I have a lot of anti-family feelings."

Back with Roger Corman, Nicholson made *The Raven*, the comedy chapter of the Poe saga with Vincent Price, Boris Karloff and Peter Lorre. *The Terror* was made with the left-over sets, costumes and cast. Corman shot three days of it; Monte Hellman did a weekend of exteriors and Francis Ford Coppola tied the whole thing together in a further eleven days. Dialogue was added as they went along; not improvised to a theme but deciding before each take what turn the storyline might take. Nicholson accepts the experience as cathartic for it awoke in him an excitement for other areas of film-making.

He began to write for the screen and the first picture to carry a credit was *Thunder Island* in 1963. "I wrote it in three weeks. It was made for 20th Century-Fox's 8-picture unit, which was just about the last 8-picture unit that ever existed. Later I did two pictures in the Philippines for them — *Back Door to Hell* and *Flight to Fury*. In a way the script for *Thunder Island* was prophetic because it dealt with an assassination and was written just before Kennedy was shot." For the other Fox pictures Nicholson was joined by Monte Hellman as director. In 1966 Hellman and Nicholson made

Opposite: The Passenger

two westerns which earned a considerable reputation. They were made back to back at a cost of 80,000 dollars each. In France they were critically acclaimed and on the festival circuit they enjoyed some success. Nicholson's old friend, Carol Eastman, wrote *The Shooting*, under her screen name of Adrien Joyce; Nicholson co-produced *The Shooting*, and wrote *Ride the Whirlwind*. He starred in both films.

"What separated them from other westerns was the level of reality in both films. Normally a western is just 'Attack at Apache Junction' and everyone gets killed and you have no chance to relate to them at all. I was into this myself at one time, for instance, in *Flight to Fury* all the characters except one are killed. But I always try to deal with violence in an honest way. I hate it when bodies just keep dropping out of the bottom of the screen and you don't feel anything. In *The Shooting* there is only one killing, at the very end, and Monte uses that jerky slow motion technique as the body falls. You used to see it a lot on television before their tape equipment got too sophisticated, and of course we had all been subjected ten thousand times to that film of Jack Ruby coming out of the crowd at Dallas. That's not to say that this is what the film is all about, but it is about the shooting of a

Right: with Stockard Channing in The Fortune. Opposite: Hell's Angels on Wheels

brother, and we just wanted to suggest it, hint at it in passing."
The Shooting is generally accepted as the better of the two
films. In it Nicholson co-starred with Millie Perkins, Warren
Oates and Will Hutchins. Nicholson plays a hired gun
commissioned by a mysterious and nameless woman to track
down and kill a person or persons unknown. The whole
action takes place in the desert, so there is the sense of chase,
or pursuit, without anything tangible being achieved. At the
end, the film answers none of the questions it poses.
"They're darned good westerns. I never felt I had to make
excuses. People would say, 'You're making a second feature.'
That's all they know. My westerns are better than a lot of
big, pretentious ones. I don't have to apologise to anyone."
In the long run, says Nicholson, he and Monte Hellman were
all but cut out of both films. "I co-produced one with him,
he directed them both, I wrote one, he edited them and I
assisted him. I promoted them and took them round the
festivals. All we got was 1,400 dollars each. For two films
and a year's work."

He played a cameo role in *The St Valentine's Day Massacre*
and stole the scene with a line of improvised dialogue. As the
chauffeur he watches a hood rubbing some foreign substance
on the ammunition and says: "It's garlic. The bullets don't
kill you, you die of blood poisoning."

His next film was *Hells Angels on Wheels* (directed by
Richard Rush) which has the dubious distinction of being the
first time the Angels gave their official permission for their
name to be used as part of the title. It was explicit, both
about drugs and violence and fell foul of the British Board of
Film Censors, as did his next film, *Psych-Out*, which he also
wrote. *Psych-Out* followed the adventures of a deaf girl who
goes to Haight Ashbury in search of her brother. Nicholson
played the leader of a rock combo who befriends her.

Another film he wrote, *The Trip*, also bothered the censors as
they felt it was likely to attract people to LSD rather than
deter them. Roger Corman directed and Peter Fonda starred.
Nicholson then wrote *Head* for The Monkees, a pop group
built up by Bob Rafelson and Bert Schneider, who directed
and produced the film. Additionally Nicholson appeared
briefly. It was a disaster, although Nicholson personally rates
it highly: "The best rock and roll movie ever made."

At the time it looked as though Jack Nicholson was destined
to remain underground forever, going from bike movies to
horror films and small budget second feature westerns.
Always the underground king fighting the established order.

*Opposite:
directing Drive,
He Said*

People talk of his amazing good fortune in being chosen to replace Rip Torn in *Easy Rider*. Certainly luck was a part of it, but there was more to it than that. The group of people involved in *Easy Rider* had been associates of Nicholson's for some time. He actually replaced Dennis Hopper years earlier at the Player's Ring Theatre when Hopper decided to go off to Mexico to learn bullfighting, and Michael Landon, the first replacement, was scooped up for television's 'Bonanza' series. Nicholson had written *The Trip* which starred Peter Fonda and Dennis Hopper. So what was more natural than that Fonda and Hopper should visit Nicholson who was writing *Head* at the time with their eight page outline for *Easy Rider*? Or that Nicholson should introduce them and it to his *Head* director and producer, Bob Rafelson and Bert Schneider. Schneider chose to become involved in *Easy Rider* — he signed a cheque for 650,000 dollars to finance it and arranged distribution with Columbia. When Hopper ran into location difficulties Nicholson introduced him to more friends from his horror/bike/western days — cameraman Laszlo Kovacs and production manager Paul Lewis (who later produced *The Last Movie* for Hopper).

It can't have come as a total surprise to Jack Nicholson when his name came up following a quarrel between Rip Torn and

*Right: with
Faye Dunaway
in Chinatown.
Opposite: Five
Easy Pieces*

Dennis Hopper which meant the part of George the lawyer was vacant. "It was the luckiest thing that ever happened to me," Nicholson says. "And it's a good film, no question about it. But maybe its great impact was on the business itself. The whole idea of spending on films, the kind of things to make for this particular audience. It caused a kind of revolution. Nicholson says he recognised that the film was different to every other bike movie that had ever been mooted. "I was one of the few people who knew it would succeed. I mean I knew a lot about the business, promotion, advertising, that kind of thing. A motor cycle movie with Peter Fonda couldn't miss, but I didn't realise how far beyond that its success would go."

Hopper and Fonda play two drop-outs who take off with some dope stashed on their motorcycles. Nicholson played a southern lawyer who suddenly decides to put on his gold football helmet and ride away on the back of Peter Fonda's motorbike. He admits that for the campfire scene — his favourite — he smoked about 155 joints. "Keeping it all in the mind stoned, and playing the scene straight and then becoming stoned — it was fantastic."

Easy Rider was a small budget road film which was a

precursor of a succession of pictures which examined the break-up of American society. The impact was instantaneous. From being a member of the underground establishment, Nicholson, virtually overnight, became recognisable to a vast audience who had never heard of *Cry Baby Killer* or *Thunder Island*. He was nominated in the Best Supporting Actor category when the Academy Awards came round.

He smiled politely when people called him an "overnight success". "If I was fifty and hadn't succeeded then I might be frustrated. But at my age it's just right. You have to be able to handle the opportunity." The new power didn't phase him either. "I've never felt any lack of power. I feel if you do the thing you'll have the power. I'm limited only by whatever my talents are."

Prior to making *Easy Rider*, he had been offered the part of Barbra Streisand's drop-out big brother figure in *On A Clear Day You Can See Forever*, Vincente Minnelli's disappointing film about extra sensory perception. At the time it had seemed like a lot of money, but it was a chore to make, one which he fulfilled following *Easy Rider*. "I hadn't really wanted to do it but two things finally persuaded me – the salary and the fact that they asked me to sing a number. I was fascinated by the idea of someone who doesn't sing doing a song. I didn't want to talk it or whisper it, and they promised me that they wouldn't dub it. They didn't, they cut it out altogether. That picture was not a happy experience for me. I was playing a rich hippie, and the first thing they told me when I turned up on the set was, get your hair cut. That was the key to the whole thing and I realised there and then what kind of time it was going to be."

However, he retrieved his reputation with *Five Easy Pieces*, written by Adrien Joyce (the pseudonym of his old friend Carol Eastman – a woman who, he says, understands him totally), and directed by another old friend, Bob Rafelson. The character was based by Adrien Joyce, half on her dead brother and half on Nicholson himself. As Bobby Dupea, Nicholson was a middle-class intellectual who drops out only to find that the alternative lifestyle is not all it's cracked up to be, either. Totally disenchanted, he returns home to visit his stricken father, hounded by the bird-brained waitress (Karen Black) who is out to marry him. Realising that his future lies with neither of them he dumps the girl at a service station and hitches a lift in the opposite direction.

Opposite: with Ann-Margret in Tommy

Another Oscar nomination, this time as Best Actor. Time magazine commented: "The role allowed Nicholson not only

to turn on his own bursting temper but to flash the charm that has its greatest single emblem in his smile." The film was very successful: not only was Nicholson nominated for Best Actor and Karen Black for Best Supporting Actress — Adrien Joyce's screenplay and the film itself were nominated. When he finished *Five Easy Pieces*, its production company, BBS — who also produced *Easy Rider* and always seemed to be around when he needed a little boost — asked if he would like to direct. "I said yes."

The vehicle he chose, *Drive, He Said*, was based on the novel by Jeremy Larner. "It was first brought to me eight years earlier, when I was young enough to have played in it. I am glad I didn't branch out into direction any earlier: it was important that I spent all that time compiling the right credentials. Directing really is a twenty-four hour a day job. I'd work, go to sleep and instantly dream about my work. Wake up the next morning and get on with it again. I hadn't realised how exhausting it would be." Nicholson gathered his friends round him among the cast — Karen Black, Bruce Dern ("He's my only real competition, Bruce, and the guy on the hill, Marlon Brando"), Robert Towne (his old room-mate) and Henry Jaglom (who would later direct him in *A Safe Place*). *Drive, He Said* was a strange mixture of draft-dodging, basketball and campus revolution. It followed the university career of Hector (William Tepper), a star of the basketball team whose truculent attitude towards the game is cramping his style because his mind is on larger issues. One

Left: with Marlon Brando in The Missouri Breaks. Opposite: Chinatown

critic commented: "Whatever the shortcomings of the script (this is not the first time that Jack Nicholson has written a subject into the ground), the direction itself is full of promise. It is an extreme film, extreme in its language, its images and its sexual explicitness, and Nicholson cuts and darts with his camera with a precision and agility that is wholly admirable. He is almost certainly going to make a much better film in the future."

The film was not generally liked and caused a furore at the Cannes Film Festival when it was shown there. "The reports of what went on at Cannes have been overblown. I was disappointed in the initial critical reaction but at least the film inspired a positive reaction. It seemed to me that the festivals would make a useful launching pad, but then I found that I was going to be spending all my time answering questions and receiving condolences. The film got pretty good reviews in the States, though." The film ran into censorship troubles about which Nicholson was stoical. "The scenes that are giving the British censor trouble do, to be fair, give people trouble everywhere. In Britain they are only asking for two or three cuts. In Canada they wanted forty. The production company who made the film — BBS — have a lot of integrity in matters like this, and they are leaving it up to me. At a certain point, one has to be reasonable about it, I suppose. A lot of people have money in the film and if it looked as though they might not get it back, I would have to give in. It's a form of blackmail, really."

Between shooting *Drive, He Said* and editing it, he went to Canada to make *Carnal Knowledge* for director Mike Nichols, an experience he thoroughly enjoyed. Written by Jules Feiffer, and co-starring Art Garfunkel, Ann-Margret and Candice Bergen, the film was a bitter and disillusioned sexual odyssey spanning twenty years in the lives of two college friends (Nicholson and Garfunkel). For the duration of *Carnal Knowledge,* Nicholson, who admitted he's been smoking cannabis every day for fifteen years, voluntarily swore off the drug to prove its non-addictive nature. He frequently talked about the need to legalise all forms of drug-taking — he has experimented with most drugs, though cannabis is the only one he takes regularly. "The only thing that disappoints me is that nothing interesting has come out of the drug culture. It's sterile. Just a lot of people sitting around looking glum, with nothing in common except that they all smoke grass."

Carnal Knowledge won rave reviews. One such read, "There

Opposite: Five Easy Pieces

has simply never been a film like *Carnal Knowledge* before: its examination of the sexual needs and frustrations of two men from their teens through to their forties is outspoken, probingly real and blisteringly honest. It seems almost ungrateful to single out performances from what is in fact a remarkable team effort, but Jack Nicholson once again proves, with this stunning portrait of a man racked by private failure, that he is one of the finest American actors about just now."

Following this, he played a cameo role as Tuesday Weld's arrogant lover in *A Safe Place*, also starring Orson Welles. The film wasn't released in England until 1975. He was reunited with director Bob Rafelson for *The King of Marvin Gardens*, co-starring another friend, Bruce Dern. "The role required him to master a more dour, slippery confessional mode," said Time magazine. "To hide his character's feelings from himself under a barrage of autobiographical patchwork. Nicholson was equal to the task. It is his most daring performance, and one of his favourites. *Marvin Gardens* asked audiences to reach out almost as far as Nicholson." Something audiences were not ready to do, and the film failed.

His next, *The Last Detail*, won him the Best Actor award at Cannes. Directed by Hal Ashby, written by Nicholson's old friend Robert Towne from a much admired novel by Darryl Ponicsan, it co-starred Randy Quaid and Otis Young, and was a tough aggressive movie about two career sailors escorting a third to a Detention Centre. During the journey the relationships between the three are built up and explored. The Pentagon were reported to be furious about the film's representation of Navy life. Said one critic: "Hal Ashby brings it brilliantly but cheerlessly to life in unremittingly bleak locations, only rarely brightened by cold winter sunshine. The three key performances are fine but, as Buddusky, Jack Nicholson steals the honours with a superbly well-rounded study. It's a flawless piece of screen acting right down, in fact, to the last detail."

Nicholson then made a nostalgic thriller, *Chinatown*, for director Roman Polanski and producer Robert Evans, with another screenplay by Robert Towne. His co-star was the elegant Faye Dunaway, as the shady lady. Nicholson played a white-suited private eye — cool, ironic, sympathetic — and the film was widely praised (another Best Actor Oscar nomination for Nicholson) though some critics commented that nostalgia wasn't what it once was. Director Polanski was surprised by Nicholson's lack of personal vanity — a rare

Opposite: with Warren Beatty in The Fortune

attribute among actors. "He simply doesn't care how he looks," Polanski says, astonished. "I put a bandage on his nose during half of *Chinatown* and he didn't object. With Jack it's only the result that counts."

The Fortune reunited Nicholson with *Carnal Knowledge* director Mike Nichols and his old friend and fellow student of female form, Warren Beatty (they have swopped girlfriends from time to time, which obviously gives them something in common). A comedy set in the '30s, it told of two scoundrels — Nicholson and Beatty — in pursuit of a young heiress (the talented Stockard Channing in her first starring role). They are determined to relieve Ms Channing of as much of her fortune as is humanly possible since its acquisition will help keep them in the style to which they would like to be accustomed. Carol Eastman (working under her real name) wrote the original screenplay and the film enjoyed a moderate success.

Nichols enjoys working with Jack Nicholson, praising the way Nicholson stimulates group feeling on the set. "I've never seen any other do it. Usually everyone has their own clique — the camera crew, electricians, and so on — but when Jack's around that feeling disappears."

Back in 1972 Nicholson had kept six months clear to work with Antonioni. "He wanted me to do a film for him in Sardinia and Brazil, but it all fell through and in the meantime I had turned something else down on the strength of it." Now Antonioni beckoned again and the film, *The Passenger*, was made. Nicholson was cast as a disenchanted television journalist who assumes the identity of a dead man he closely resembles. Once the pose is struck he finds himself doubly trapped because the dead man was a dealer in armaments, committed to a programme of appointments and deals that the imposter must keep. Despite several hiccoughs during production and on the way to an opening date, *The Passenger* finally received the homage of the critics, who felt it marked Antonioni's return to form after the disappointing *Zabriskie Point*. Nicholson was superb, assisted by the intriguing Maria Schneider as a wayward hitch-hiker.

Nicholson finally got his chance to sing on screen in Ken Russell's version of The Who's rock opera, *Tommy*. He played a small role of a specialist who is consulted to heal blind, deaf and dumb Tommy. The film, which starred Roger Daltrey, Ann-Margret and Oliver Reed, was an enormous success. "The visual aspect of the film is superb — a hose jet of images that are literally stunning in their impact. Rarely

Opposite: One Flew Over the Cuckoo's Nest

LARAMIE JUNIOR HIGH IMC

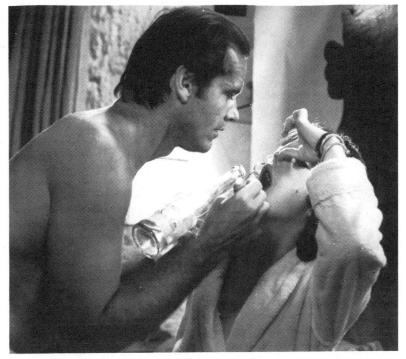

Left: with Maria Schneider in The Passenger. Opposite: with Barbra Streisand in On a Clear Day You Can See Forever

has a film been designed with such dramatic unity without becoming overly self-conscious. Jack Nicholson is fine as the serpentine specialist to whom Tommy is taken," one critic observed.

And so to *One Flew Over the Cuckoo's Nest* which in 1976 won Jack Nicholson the Best Actor Oscar he'd been chasing so long. In fact *Cuckoo's Nest* swept the Oscars that year, winning Best Film, Best Director (Milos Forman), Best Actress (Louis Fletcher), Best Screenplay (Lawrence Hauben, Bo Goldman). The following year it similarly dominated the BAFTA awards, winning Best Actor, Best Actress, Best Supporting Actor (Brad Dourif), Best Film, Best Director, Best Editing (Richard Chew, Lynzee Klingman, Sheldon Kahn). Ken Kesey's 1963 novel had been bought for the screen by Kirk Douglas, who played the leading role on Broadway. For years Douglas tried to raise money to finance the movie without success. Finally he gave it as a birthday present to his son Michael, but he kept a small percentage. Michael Douglas packaged the film, signing Milos Forman to direct and assembling a cast with only Nicholson as a name actor. Nicholson plays McMurphy, serving a prison term for statutory rape, who goes for what he considers a soft option

of the psychiatric wing. The film was almost wholly set in a mental asylum where McMurphy bursts into the ordered calm of the ward, the passionate voice crying out against the Establishment who equate non-conformity with madness. To the post Vietnam America the film was cathartic, and its appeal was universal.

Since *Cuckoo's Nest* Nicholson has made *The Missouri Breaks* for director Arthur Penn, co-starring Marlon Brando. A disappointing western with Brando as a bounty killer and Nicholson as the leader of the rustlers he's hired to catch. "Heaven knows what three very talented people saw in this one," commented one reviewer. Following this Nicholson made an appearance in another disappointing film, Elia Kazan's *The Last Tycoon*, based on F Scott Fitzgerald's last unfinished book, and written for the screen by Harold Pinter. Nicholson was excellent as a Union boss hounding Hollywood mogul — and central character — Monroe Stahr (the impressive Robert DeNiro), said to be based by Fitzgerald on Irving Thalberg. Among the cast was Jeff Corey, the man who ran the drama school in which Nicholson first served his apprenticeship.

Clearly Jack Nicholson has now become a senior citizen of

the angry actors. A new breed of non-conformists, Al Pacino, Robert DeNiro, Richard Dreyfuss among them, are pushing the boundaries Nicholson established still further. "The system is geared towards overworking the stars. There aren't that many around to haul the freight." He has come a long way – from 1,400 dollars a year to 750,000 plus profits per film, but he can't escape the feeling that acting is a childish thing to do. "There's something in the instinctive actor that is infantile. Everyone has that streak, but actors make use of it." He has a short temper, but loses it less frequently now than in the past. "I have to blow my top now and then, throw a tantrum. All right, so it's not nice but no-one's going to give you an Oscar because you were nice to work with – only for what comes out on the screen. You're the only one who has to give the performance and you give it the best way you can."

And if you want a thumbnail sketch of his life, he's willing to oblige: "I read, swim, go out, have love affairs."

He lives in Hollywood in the same apartment block as Marlon Brando, usually with Anjelica Huston, the daughter of director John Huston. The front door is always open for friends and the three telephones are usually ringing. There he reads the International Herald Tribune, and collects effigies of pigs – stuffed toy pigs, carved wooden pigs. "When pigs became the symbol of evil I adopted them," he says, by way of explanation. His two great pleasures are dope and women, although he once admitted, "I'd much rather win an Oscar than a pretty girl. One is permanent and the other is not." As far as screen acting is concerned, he is utterly diligent. Not only does he underline key phrases and make notes on his script, he also assigns numbers to almost every word, signifying beats and pauses. "I try to find a character's positive philosophy about himself," he says.

Success hasn't really altered him. "Money, as someone once said, isn't everything. The very first year I started making movies I earned 1,400 dollars which, in America is like earning nothing at all. But I survived. I was happy. I knew I'd make it some day and that gave me the courage to hang on. What I didn't expect to happen was to find myself a superstar in the same league as Paul Newman and Robert Redford. I can't believe there are always chauffeured limousines waiting at my beck and call and that other people are always ready to pick up the cheque." And he is a realist. "Once they want you, you can be certain the day will come when they won't any more."

Opposite: The Missouri Breaks

Filmography

CRY BABY KILLER
US 1958

Producers/David Kramarsky, David March. Director/Jus Addiss. Script/Leo Gordon, Melvin Levy. Music/Gerald Fried. Photography/Floyd Crosby. B&W. GB disyribution/Associated British-Pathe. Certificate A. 59 mins.

With: Harry Lauter (Porter), Jack Nicholson (Jimmy), Carolyn Mitchell (Carole), Brett Halsey (Manny), Lynn Cartwright (Julie), Ralph Reed (Joey), John Shay (Gannon)

TOO SOON TO LOVE
US 1959

Producer-director/Richard Rush. Script/ Richard Rush, Laszlo Gorog. Music/ Ronald Stein. B&W. GB distribution/ none. No certificate. 85 mins.

With: Jennifer West, Richard Evans, Warren Parker, Ralph Manza, Jack Nicholson

THE WILD RIDE
US 1960

Producer-director/Roger Corman. GB distribution/none. No certificate. 80 mins.

With: Jack Nicholson, Georgianna Carter, Robert Bean

STUDS LONIGAN
US 1960

Producer/Philip Yordan. Director/ Irving Lerner. Script/Philip Yordan. Music/Gerrald Goldsmith. Photography/ Arthur H Fiendel. B&W. GB distribution/United Artists. Certificate X. 103 mins (GB: 95 mins)

With: Christopher Knight (Studs Lonigan), Frank Gorshin (Kenny Killarney), Venetia Stevenson (Lucy Scanlon), Carolyn Craig (Catherine Banahan), Jack Nicholson (Weary Riley), Robert Caper (Paulie Haggerty), Dick Foran (Patrick Lonigan), Katherine Square (Mrs Lonigan), Jay C Flippen (Father Gilhooey)

THE LITTLE SHOP OF HORRORS
US 1960

Producer - director / Roger Corman. Script/Charles B Griffith. Music/Fred Katz. Photography/Arch Dalzell. B&W. GB distribution/Hemdale. Certificate A. 70 mins.

With: Jonathan Haze (Seymour Krelboind),Jackie Joseph (Audrey), Mel Welles (Gravis Mushnick), Dick Miller (Fouch), Myrtle Vail (Winifred), Leola Wendorff (Mrs Shiva), Jack Nicholson (Wilbur Force)

THE BROKEN LAND
US 1961

Producer/Leonard A Schwartz. Director/ John Bushelman. Script/Edward Lakso. Music/Richard LaSalle. Photography/ Floyd Crosby. B&W. GB distribution/ 20th Century-Fox. Certificate A. 59 mins.

With: Kent Taylor (Jim Kogan), Dianna Darrin (Mavra Aikens), Jody McCrea (Ed Flynn), Robert Sampson (Gabe Dunson), Jack Nicholson (Will Broicous), Gary Snead (Billy Bell)

THUNDER ISLAND
US 1963

Producer-director/Jack Leewood. Scr/ Don Devlin, Jack Nicholson. Music/ Paul Sawtell, Bert Shefter. Photography/John Nickolaus Jnr. B&W. GB distribution/20th Century-Fox. Certificate U. 65 mins.

With: Gene Nelson (Billy Poole), Fay Spain (Helen Dodge), Brian Kelly (Vincent Dodge), Miriam Colon (Anita Chavez), Art Bedard (Ramon Alou), Antonio Torres Martino (Colonel Cepeda), Esther Sandoval (Rena), Jose De San Anton (Antonio Perez), Evelyn Kaufman (Jo Dodge), Stephanie Rifkinson (Linda Perez)

THE RAVEN
US 1963

Producer - director / Roger Corman. Script/Richard Matheson. Music/Les Baxter. Photography/Floyd Crosby. Pathecolor. GB distribution/EMI. Certificate X. 86 mins.

With: Vincent Price (Dr Erasmus Craven), Peter Lorre (Dr Bedlo), Boris Karloff (Dr Scarabus), Jazel Court (Lenore Craven), Olive Sturgess (Estelle Craven), Jack Nicholson (Rexford Craven), Connie Wallace (Maidservant), William Baskin (Grimes), Aaron Saxon (Gort)

THE TERROR
US 1963

Producer - director / Roger Corman. Script/Leo Gordon, Jack Hill. Music/ Ronald Stein. Photography/John Nickolaus. Pathecolor. GB distribution/ Grand National. Certificate X. 81 mins.

With: Boris Karloff (Baron von Leppe), Jack Nicholson (Andre Duvalier),

Sandra Knight (Helene), Richard Miller (Stefan), Dorothy Neumann (Witch Woman), Jonathan Haze (Gustaf)

ENSIGN PULVER
US 1964

Producer-director/Joshua Logan. Script/ Joshua Logan, Peter S Feibleman. Music/George Duning. Photography/ Charles Lawton. Colour. GB distribution/Warner-Pathe. Certificate A. 83 mins.

With: Robert Walker Jnr, Burl Ives, Walter Matthau, Tommy Sands, Millie Perkins, Kay Medford, Larry Hagman, Jack Nicholson, Al Freeman Jnr, James Farentino, James Coco

BACK DOOR TO HELL
US/Philippines 1964

Producer/Fred Roos. Director/Monte Hellman. Script/Richard A Guttman, John Hackett. Music/Mike Velarde. Photography/Mars Rasca. B&W. GB distribution/20th Century-Fox. Certificate A. 69 mins.

With: Jimmie Rodgers (Lieutenant Craig), Jack Nicholson (Burnett), John Hackett (Jersey), Annabelle Huggins (Maria), Conrad Maga (Paco), Johnny Monteiro (Ramundo).

FLIGHT TO FURY
US 1965

Director/Monte Hellman. Scr/Jack Nicholson. GB distribution/none. 80 mins.

With: Dewey Martin, Fay Spain, Vic Diaz.

THE SHOOTING
US 1966

Producers/Jack Nicholson, Monte Hellman. Director/Monte Hellman. Scr/Adrien Joyce. Music/Richard Markowitz. Photography/Gregory Sandor. Colour by DeLuxe. GB distribution/Ember. Certificate A. 81 mins.

With: Warren Oates (Willet Gashade), Will Hutchins (Coley), Millie Perkins (Woman), Jack Nicholson (Billy Spear), B J Merholz (Leland Drum), Cuy El Tsosie (Indian), Charles Eastman (Bearded Man)

RIDE THE WHIRLWIND
US 1966

Director/Monte Hellman. Scr/Jack Nicholson. Colour. GB distribution/ none.

With: Cameron Mitchell, Jack Nicholson, Tom Filer, Millie Perkins

Below: director of Drive, He Said

HELL'S ANGELS ON WHEELS
US 1967

Director/Richard Rush. Script/Jack Nicholson. GB distribution/Antony Balch (unreleased). Certificate X (issued 13.5.77). 95 mins.

With: Adam Roarke, Jack Nicholson, Sabrina Scharf, Jana Taylor, John Garwood

THE TRIP
US 1967

Producer - director / Roger Corman. Script/Jack Nicholson. Music/The Electric Flag. Photography/Arch Dalzell. Pathecolor. GB distribution/ none. Certificate not issued. 85 mins.

With: Peter Fonda (Paul Groves), Susan Strasberg (Sally), Bruce Dern (John), Dennis Hopper (Max), Salli Sachse (Glenn), Katherine Walsh (Lulu), Barboura Morris (Flo), Caren Bernsen (Alexandra), Dick Miller (Cash), Luana Anders (Waitress)

PSYCHO-OUT
US 1968

Producer/Dick Clark. Director/Richard Rush. Script/E Hunter Willett, Betty Ulius. Music/various. Photography/ Laszlo Kovacs. Pathecolor. GB distribution/Promotion Pictures. Certificate X. 88 mins.

With: Susan Strasberg (Jennie), Dean Stockwell (Dave), Jack Nicholson (Stoney), Bruce Dern (Steve), Adam Roarke (Ben), Max Julien (Elwood), Robert Kelljan (Arthur), Henry Jaglom (Warren), Barbara London (Sadie), Tommy Flanders (Wesley)

HEAD
US 1968

Director/Bob Rafelson. Scr/Jack Nicholson. Colour. GB distribution/ Columbia (unreleased). Certificate A. 85 mins.

With: The Monkees (Micky Dolenz, Davy Jones, Mike Nesmith, Peter Tork), Victor Mature, Sonny Liston, Ray Nitschke, June Fairchild

EASY RIDER
US 1969

Producer/Peter Fonda. Director/Dennis Hopper. Script/Peter Fonda, Dennis Hopper, Terry Southern. Music/various. Photography/Laszlo Kovacs, Technicolor. GB distribution/Columbia-Warner (Columbia). Certificate X. 95 mins.

With: Peter Fonda (Wyatt), Dennis Hopper (Billy), Antonio Mendoza (Jesus), Phil Spector (Connection), Mac Mashourian (Body Guard), Warren Finnerty (Rancher), Luke Askew (Stranger), Luana Anders (Stranger), Sabrina Scharf (Sarah), Robert Walker (Jack), Jack Nicholson (George Hanson), Toni Basil (Mary), Karen Marmer (Karen)

DRIVE, HE SAID
US 1970

Producers/Steve Blaunder, Jack Nicholson. Director/Jack Nicholson. Script/ Jeremy Larner, Jack Nicholson. Music/ David Shire. Photography/Bill Butler. Colour. GB distribution/Columbia-Warner (Columbia), Certificate X. 90 mins.

With: William Tepper (Hector Bloom), Karen Black (Olive), Michael Margotta (Gabriel), Bruce Dern (Coach Bullion), Robert Towne (Richard Clavin), Henry Jaglom (Professor Conrad), Mike Warren (Easly), June Fairchild (Sylvie Mertens), Don Hanmer (Director of Athletics), Lynn Bernay (Dance Instructor)

Opposite: Easy Rider

ON A CLEAR DAY YOU CAN SEE FOREVER
US 1970

Producer/Howard W Koch. Director/ Vincente Minnelli. Script/Alan Jay Lerner. Music/Burton Lane. Photography/Harry Stradling. Technicolor. GB distribution/CIC (Paramount). Certificate U. 130 mins.

With: Barbra Streisand (Daisy Gamble), Yves Montand (Dr Marc Chabot), Bob Newhart (Dr Mason Hume), Larry Blyden (Warren Pratt), Simon Oakland (Dr Conrad Fuller), Jack Nicholson (Tad Pringle), John Richardson (Robert Tentrees), Pamela Browne (Mrs Fitzherbert), Irene Handl (Winnie Wainwhisle), Roy Kinnear (Prince Regent)

CARNAL KNOWLEDGE
US 1971

Producer-director/Mike Nichols. Script/ Jules Feiffer. Music/various. Photography/Giuseppe Rotunno. Technicolor. GB distribution/20th Century-Fox. Certificate X. 97 mins.

With: Jack Nicholson (Jonathan), Candice Bergen (Susan), Arthur Garfunkel (Sandy), Ann-Margret (Bobbie), Rita Moreno (Louise), Cynthia O'Neal (Cindy), Carol Kane (Jennifer)

A SAFE PLACE
US 1971

Producer/Bert Schneider. Director-script/Henry Jaglom. Music/Jim Gitter. Photography/Dick Kratina. Technicolor. GB distribution/Pleasant Pastures. Certificate AA. 92 mins.

With: Tuesday Weld (Noah/Susan), Jack Nicholson (Mitch), Orson Welles (Magician), Philip Proctor (Fred), Gwen Welles (Bari), Dov Lawrence (Larry), Fanny Birkenmaier (Maid)

FIVE EASY PEICES
US 1970

Producers/Bob Rafelson, Richard Wechsler. Director/Bob Rafelson. Scr/ Adrien Joyce. Music/various. Photography/Laszlo Kovacs. Technicolor. GB distribution / Columbia - Warner (Columbia). Certificate AA. 98 mins.

With: Jack Nicholson (Robert Eroica Dupea), Karen Black (Rayette Dipesto), Lois Smith (Partita Dupea), Susan Anspach (Catherine Van Ost), Billy "Green" Bush (Elton), Fannie Flagg (Stoney), Ralph Waite (Carl Fidelio Dupea), Helena Kallianiotes (Palm Apodaca), Toni Basil (Terry Grouse), Sally Ann Struthers (Betty)

THE KING OF MARVIN GARDENS
US 1972

Producer-director/Bob Rafelson. Script/ Jacob Brackman. Music/Synchrofilm Inc. Photography/Laszlo Kovacs. Eastman Colour. GB distribution/ Columbia-Warner (Columbia). Certificate X. 104 mins.

With: Jack Nicholson (David Staebler), Bruce Dern (Jason Staebler), Ellen Burstyn (Sally), Julia Anne Robinson (Jessica), Benjamin "Scatman" Crothers (Lewis), Charles Lavine (Grandfather), Arnold Williams (Rosko), John Ryan (Surtees)

Opposite: Carnal Knowledge

THE FORTUNE
US 1974

Producers/Mike Nichols, Don Devlin.
Director/Mike Nichols. Scr/Adrien
Joyce. Music/David Shire. Photography/
John A Alonzo. Technicolor. GB distri-
bution/Columbia-Warner (Columbia).
Certificate AA. 88 mins.

With: Jack Nicholson (Oscar Sullivan),
Warren Beatty (Nicky Stumpo),
Stockard Channing (Fredricka Quintessa
Bigard), Florence Stanley (Mrs Gould),
Richard B Shull (Chief Detective),
Tom Newman (John the Barber), John
Fiedler (Police Photographer), Scatman
Crothers (Fisherman), Dub Taylor
(Rattlesnake Tom)

THE LAST DETAIL
US 1973

Producer/Gerald Ayres. Director/Hal
Ashby. Script/Robert Towne. Music/
Johnny Mandel. Photography/Michael
Chapman. Metrocolor. GB distribution/
Columbia-Warner (Columbia). Certifi-
cate X. 104 mins.

With: Jack Nicholson (Billy "Bad Ass"
Buddusky), Otis Young ("Mule"
Mulhall), Randy Quaid (Larry
Meadows), Clifton James (M.A.A.),
Carol Kane (Young Whore), Michael
Moriarty (Marine O.D.), Luana Anders
(Donna), Kathleen Miller (Annette)

CHINATOWN
US 1974

Producer/Robert Evans. Director/
Roman Polanski. Script/Robert Towne.
Music/Jerry Goldsmith. Photography/
John A Alonzo. Technicolor. GB
distribution/CIC (Paramount). Certifi-
cate X. 131 mins.

With: Jack Nicholson (J J Gittes), Faye
Dunaway (Evelyn Mulwray), John
Huston (Noah Cross), Perry Lopez
(Escobar), John Hillerman (Yelburton),
Darrell Zwerling (Hollis Mulwray),
Diane Ladd (Ida Sessions), Roy Jenson
(Mulvihill), Roman Polanski (Man With
Knife)

PROFESSIONE: REPORTER
(GB: THE PASSENGER)
Italy/France/Spain 1975

Producer / Carlo Ponti. Director /
Michelangelo Antonioni. Script/Mark
Peploe. Music/Ivan Vandor. Pho-
tography/Luciano Tovoli. Metrocolor.
GB distribution/CIC (MGM). Certificate
A. 119 mins.

With: Jack Nicholson (David Locke),
Maria Schneider (Girl), Jenny Runacre
(Rachel Locke), Ian Hendry (Martin
Knight), Stephen Berkoff (Stephen),
Ambrose Bia (Achebe), Jose Maria
Carafel (Hotel Keeper), James Campbell
(Witch Doctor), Manfred Spies (German
Stranger)

Opposite:
The Fortune

TOMMY
GB 1975

Producers/Robert Stigwood, Ken Russell. Director-script/Ken Russell. Music/Pete Townshend and The Who. Photography/Dick Bush, Ronnie Taylor. Colour. GB distribution/ Hemdale. Certificate AA. 108 mins.

With: Ann-Margret (Nora Walker), Oliver Reed (Frank Hobbs), Roger Daltrey (Tommy), Elton John (Pinball Wizard), Eric Clapton (Preacher), Keith Moon (Uncle Ernie), Jack Nicholson (Doctor), Robert Powell (Group Captain Walker), Paul Nicholas (Cousin Kevin), Tina Turner (Acid Queen), Barry Winch (Young Tommy)

THE MISSOURI BREAKS
US 1976

Producer/Robert M. Sherman. Director/ Arthur Penn. Script/Thomas McGuane. Music/John Williams. Photography/ Michael Butler. Colour by DeLuxe. GB distribution/United Artists. Certificate AA. 126 mins.

With: Marlon Brando (Robert Lee Clayton), Jack Nicholson (Tom Logan), Randy Quaid (Little Tod), Kathleen Lloyd (Jane Braxton), Frederic Forrest (Cary), Harry Dean Stanton (Calvin), John McLiam (David Braxton), John Ryan (Si), Sam Gilman (Hank Rate)

THE LAST TYCOON
US 1976

Producer/Sam Spiegel. Director/Elia Kazan. Script/Harold Pinter. Music/ Maurice Jarre. Photography/Victor Kemper. Technicolor. GB distribution/ CIC (Paramount). Certificate AA. 124 mins.

With: Robert DeNiro (Monroe Stahr), Tony Curtis (Rodriguez), Robert Mitchum (Pat Brady), Jeanne Moreau (Didi), Jack Nicholson (Brimmer), Donald Pleasence (Boxley), Ingrid Boulting (Kathleen Moore), Ray Milland (Fleishacker), Dana Andrews (Red Ridingwood), Theresa Russell (Cecilia Brady), Peter Strauss (Wylie), Tige Andrews (Popolos), Morgan Farley (Marcus), John Carradine (Guide), Jeff Corey (Doctor), Diane Shalet (Stahr's Secretary), Seymour Cassel (Seal Trainer), Angelica Huston (Edna)

ONE FLEW OVER THE CUKOO'S NEST
US 1975

Producers/Saul Zaentz, Michael Douglas. Director/Milos Forman. Script/Lawrence Hauben, Bo Goldman. Music/Jack Nitzsche. Photography/ Haskell Wexler. Colour by DeLuxe. GB distribution/United Artists. Certificate X. 134 mins.

With: Jack Nicholson (Randall P McMurphy), Louise Fletcher (Nurse Ratched), William Redfield (Harding), Will Sampson (Chief Bromden), Brad Dourif (Billy Bibbit), Sydney Lassick (Cheswick), Christopher Lloyd (Taber), Danny De Vito (Martini)

Opposite:
The Last
Tycoon

First published in Great Britain in
1977 by
BCW PUBLISHING LIMITED

© BCW Publishing Ltd. 1977

ACKNOWLEDGMENTS
We would like to thank the following
people and film companies for their
help and permission to reproduce
photographs:
CIC (UK) Limited
Columbia-Warner Distributors
Hemdale
20th Century-Fox
United Artists Corporation
and the staff of the Information
Department of the British Film
Institute

Front cover: Tommy
Frontispiece: The Last Detail

About The General Editor

DAVID CASTELL was born in London in 1943 and educated at Dulwich College. He worked first in advertising, then in magazine journalism. He had contributed film reviews to *The Times Educational Supplement, Illustrated London News*, and *London Life* before, with John Williams, he co-founded the monthly magazine *Films Illustrated* in 1971. After that came BCW Publishing, a company specializing in cinema topics. Mr. Castell reviews regularly for Capital Radio, London's leading commercial station, and was resident host of the BBC television program "Film Night." He contributes writings on cinema to a variety of newspapers and magazines, including the *Sunday Telegraph*. The fourth in a series of annuals he edits, *Cinema '79*, has just been published in the United States.

About The Author

BRUCE BRAITHWAITE contributes writings on films to several British newspapers, and has one of the country's largest collection of original campaign books, stills, and press material. He is currently working with Joanna Campbell on "The Godfather and his Sons," a genealogy of directors who have worked for, and under the patronage of, Francis Ford Coppola.

DATE DUE

FEB 29 1996		
MAR 2 1 1996		
DEC - 5 1996		